A Little Bit of Betty

BETTY A. HUNTER

A Little Bit of Betty
Copyright © 2019 by Betty A. Hunter

Tellwell Talent
www.tellwell.ca

ISBN
978-0-2288-0403-1 (Hardcover)
978-0-2288-0402-4 (Paperback)
978-0-2288-0404-8 (eBook)

I dedicate this book to my three sons,
my two grand-daughters and my
best friend, my husband.

Dear Betty,

Congratulations! You have some really strong poems here. I thoroughly enjoyed reading them. From silly and funny to sad and profound, your poems run the full gamut. There's something here for everyone. And, the fact that you bravely wrote about the loss of your son is admirable. It will help readers who are dealing with their own loss and serve as a reminder to all of us to celebrate life and those around us.

I wish you all the best as you continue on your journey with this project.

Kind Regards,

Ann Marie Downey
Your Tellwell Editor

Table of Contents

Photos taken by Betty and Curtis Hunter

Laugh A Little

A Fart

I once was called a little fart.
Then one day I took it to heart.
They can be a real stinker or as quiet as a thinker.
They can be young or even old,
But either way they're rude I'm told.

They can be dry and a little squeaky.
They can be wet and a little leaky.
I heard a fart during church one day.
That was the funniest I must say.

When Grandma walks she farts and toots.
She cannot hear them, so who gives a hoot.
They can be silent and clear a room
Or go off with a great big boom.

I think a dog fart is the worst kind.
It will gag and choke you, you will find.
Now a cat fart is a different story.
It has its very own category.

A weapon to the masses
Comes out their furry asses.
Oh no … my eyes are burning,
And there he sits with his motor purring.

Everybody has them
In levels of degrees,
So I think I must carry
My bottle of "Febreeze."

Beach Babe

Lazing in the noon-day sun,
This beach babe's gonna have fun.
The water's so fine,
And I'll drink some wine,
Lazing in the noon-day sun.

I know I can be a brat
When I wear my big sun hat.
My bikini's shiny and gold
And I've been told that I'm too old
To go bathing in the noon-day sun.

I drank up all of my booze
And had me a little snooze.
Woke up to boys, making so much noise.
My bikini had slipped
And out fell my naughty bits.
They're gazing at the noon-day sun.

Now it puts me in the mood
To sun bathe in the nude.
Put on my sunscreen; listen to the boys scream.
I'll go skipping and skinny dipping.
I'm a floating in the noon-day sun.

Well I woke up on my back
With a chest full of cold packs.
The EMTs were on their knees
Putting salve on my Double D's.
No more lazing in the sun for me!
No, no … more lazing in the sun for me!

Boobs

For your birthday
I wanted to buy you a new set of boobs,
But they only had some long-like tubes.
Now I know you can be a little quirky
So wanted to find you some that were perky.

I called the "Boob Fairy" just to see,
But she only had weird ones that came in three's.
So she gave me a number I could call,
But the boob on the phone wasn't helpful at all.

He was an idiot. That's all I can say.
He only had green ones in stock that day.
So you have to be happy with what you got.
I really tried hard … did I not?

Big ones are very overrated
And their price tags are highly inflated.
You're still loved my friend, no matter what.
You may be getting old, but you'll always be "hot."

Little Drummer Boy

He crawls over to the Tupperware on the floor.
He bangs the wooden spoon on a bowl.
My eyes twitch and my head starts to pound.
Stop! You're driving me crazy!

He bangs on his toy drum
As he marches around the house.
That really was a bad idea …
Stop! You're driving me crazy!

He does his homework at the table.
His pencils are playing a constant tattoo.
Quit tapping and do your homework!
Oh my God, he's driving me crazy!

Teenagers are hard to buy for.
He wants drums for Christmas.
I know this isn't going to be good …
Oh my God, he's driving me crazy!

Hey Mom, we are starting a band.
Not in our house. No way, Jose!
The drums are now in a friend's basement …
Thank God. Silence at last!

Hey Mom, come see our band at the bar.
Yeah, okay … this might be fun.
Well, holy cow, he's amazing! That's my boy!
Standing ovation as tears of pride stream down my face …

I knew he was a drummer!
I gave him his first drum!
See, I knew what I was doing!
I must have the patience of a saint!

My Canada

B.C.'s got tree huggers and hippies growing pot,
Joining up with Green Peace, protesting on the spot.
Then over the Rockies are the rednecks of Alberta
Driving all their big-ass trucks; gas and oil has no quota.
Pump-jacks working steady day and night.
Aurora Borealis is another common site.

Then the farmers of our Prairies,
Every year they sweat and toil:
Milking cows, planting crops,
Praying for perfect weather
Over that deep rich soil.

Ontario has politics
With big wigs who are Big Dicks,
Thinking how to spend
All this country's dough,
Forever making cutbacks,
Taxing the poor average Joe.

Now Quebec's the crazy Province.
I don't know what to say.
You have to speak their language –
Only French ... NO ENGLAIS!

Maritimes are marvelous. There's beauty everywhere.
Warm hearts of the people, show you that they care.
And when the jobs were gone, they left it in a hurry,
Packed up all their stuff
And moved to Ft. McMurray.

My Twisted Side

When people first meet me,
They see the gracious lady I am.
And if they really get to know me,
My mouth turns into spam.

Sometimes I just can't help myself.
My favourite word is "shit."
I said it once in church,
And it was a funny hit.

I like to see the shock on faces.
It is so much fun.
They had me pegged all wrong,
And like a taser I will stun.

I am quick witted
And will be sure to make you smile.
Come sit beside me, and you'll laugh
your ass off for a while.

I called my boys all dickheads
and friends were shocked and amazed.
They turned out funny and fabulous,
those dickheads that I raised.

So my friends I'll tell you now,
don't judge a book by its cover.
You may be pleasantly surprised
when we get to know one another.

Next Question Please

Can an ass be an asshole?
Can a donkey be as stubborn as a mule?
Can a skunk smell his odious odour?
Can ice cream melt but still be cool?

Can time stand still when you're still standing?
Can you answer a question with only a stare?
Can a horse be hoarse?
Can a hare have hair?

Can a pretty face have an ugly heart?
Can a wise man be a fool?
Can you judge a man by his wealth?
Can you measure the golden rule?

Can you speak without talking?
Can you see without eyes?
Can you hear the sun rising?
Can you touch clear blue skies?

Can you answer a question with a question?
Can you see beyond the grave?
Can you care enough to be selfless?
Can you be scared and yet be brave?

Can you read between the lines?
Can your thoughts be heard?
Can you exist on a different plane?
Can you be odd without being weird?

Oh Shit

Amazing Shit, Big Shit
And Bullshit went to a party
To stir up a little shit
At Crazy Shit's place.

Dipshit, Deep Shit and Good Shit
Were already there
But didn't give a shit
When Holy Shit, King Shit and
    Little Shit arrived.

Major Shit walked in
but had no shit, so
Queer Shit began to
Shoot the shit with him.

When Special Shit
And Silly Shit were
    acting stupid,
Sure as shit,
Shit Balls staggered in totally shit-faced.

Then the fun began,
when Shithead and Serious Shit
Had a Shit storm in the shit house
And both fell into the shit hole.

They both got a shit kicking
From Shit on a Stick
Over their stupid shit.
And he taught them this lesson …

If you stir the shit-pot … you have to lick the spoon!
Oh SHIT!

Perfect Recipe

INGREDIENTS:

Love	Trust
Patience	Understanding
Compassion	Acceptance
Tolerance	Willingness
Self-sacrifice	Compromise
Thankfulness	Forgiveness
Graciousness	Harmony

Marinate together two very tender hearts.
Sear over high heat to seal in the deep savoury flavours.
Gently sauté in a sauce made from undying love and commitment.
Simmer with a dash of dreams and sweet moments.

Pour a little sweet and sour sauce over it to ensure the deepest
    rich flavours.
Add a few dashes of hot spice to give it zest.
Cook for a few years until the two hearts have become one.

Now place yourselves on the back burner on low for several years,
While you knead and nurture the fruit of your loins,
Stirring gently for the fullest, richest experience.

Put all ingredients into a pressure cooker for faster results
Or one may prefer the slow-cooker method.
Either way, results come out the same.

Some sections will be extremely tender and delicious,
While others will be tough, chewy and hard to swallow.

Try to keep an even temperature for best results.
Baste often to ensure greatest tenderness.
Don't overcook or the juices will dry out.

When done to your satisfaction, turn off the elements,
Sit back and enjoy the delightful deliciousness of your success.

Reward yourselves by pairing it with a deep-bodied wine aged
to perfection.
Serve on finest china and savour the flavour of the experience.

Let the succulence of the secret ingredients enliven your souls,
As it gently flows over your taste buds in its entirety.
Relax and enjoy each other by romantic candlelight and soft music.

Pillow Talk

If you have a problem with your fellow,
Just remember there's always the pillow.
A girl can only take so much o'er the years.
Men drive you crazy and you end up in tears.

Keep your cool and have a glass of wine.
Take a deep breath. You'll know when it's time.
Count to three and if that doesn't work
Just use the pillow on the big jerk.

The size doesn't matter. It's all about the pressure.
Hold it real tight now and you'll soon have some pleasure.
Your troubles will ease and you'll begin to smile.
Don't hesitate … you'll be just fine in a while.

Am I going mad? What the hell am I thinking?
My horrible daydreams are enough to start me drinking!
Oh shit, what am I saying … Where's my rye?
To hell with him. I'll just say goodbye.

I'd take the car, but it's run out of gas.
Plus the keys are now dangling out of his ass!
I think I'm leaving now, so I can finally be free.
I'll just pack my bags and take my pillow with me!

Inspirational

Butterfly

She has been wrapped in silk for much of her life.
The stirrings of something new begin to arouse her.
She slowly struggles to relieve herself of her old form.
She emerges at last and sheds the shroud that held her captive for
    so long.

She appears with her new wings of purpose still damp.
She then flutters them dry in the warmth of the sun.
Her beauty is stunning and she is ready to fly.
She is new. She is freshly born. She is complete.

She is ready to try out her new wings.
She flutters once, twice, then suddenly she is gone –
Gone to where destiny beckons her.

Upon the breeze that gently blows her in the right direction,
She travels beyond the rose-scented gardens
To a land that seems endless with skies forever more.
She is free at last from the tomb of the past.

Her energy splashes beauty across long-forgotten paths.
Her touch upon the velvet petals is softer than the kiss of a fairy.
The shape and colours of her wings form her new identity.
She feels whole with her newness, and she will now be enough:
Enough to carry her through on uncharted flights,
Into the future of her short cycle of life.

Camper's Lullaby

A butterfly flutters by.
A hummer's wings are humming.
Birds feed at the feeders.
The garden fountain's pumping.

Dragonflies are flying past
As songbirds sing their songs.
Tomatoes ripen on the vine.
Now the sprinkler sputters on.

Summertime's the time for me.
I like barbeques and steak.
I go where swimmers like to swim
And relax out on the lake.

Looking from the lookout,
Perched upon the hill,
The view up there is breathless.
The climb is worth the thrill.

As northern lights begin to dance
Their dance across the sky,
The owls hoot and coyotes sing
The camper's lullaby.

The Carousel of Life

This journey of life has its ups and downs
Like a pony on a merry-go-round.
We are always changing, never the same.
Our wounds and scars each have a name.

Some days are hard and some are better.
I never give up because I'm no quitter.
I just push forward one day at a time.
This is my mountain I have to climb.

Don't look behind, but focus ahead.
Bring healing energy to hurts instead.
Only you can change your outlook on things.
Look for the good and see the spirit it brings.

Spread love with kindness, in thought and deed.
You may have saved a soul or be the answer to a need.
We cannot judge what we see by sight.
Who sees you crying in the middle of the night?

Say good morning as you greet the day.
Take a deep breath and blow your troubles away.
Positive energy can bring us peace of mind.
It doesn't cost a penny just to smile and be kind.

What is your purpose in this world of despair?
Who will know or remember you once were there?
Your soul is connected to a plan we cannot see.
One day we'll find out, and know it wasn't just about me …

Cleansing

You can smell it in the air when the rain is coming.
I like it when it rains at night.
As I listen, I hear it beating against the windows,
And it makes a steady rhythm on the roof.
I especially enjoy a good thunderstorm:
With it brings memories of when I was a kid.

I would watch from my window and listen.
The sky would rumble out its anger from the dark, heavy clouds.
And then the amazing lightning show would begin.
One Mississippi, two Mississippi, three Mississippi, BANG!
Wow that one was close.

Somehow during this turmoil in the night sky, I'd find peace –
Peace in knowing it would pass.
I'd close my eyes and breathe in the earthy aroma
Which would arise from the freshly watered ground.
And washed clean would be the corners of Mother Nature's dusty house
Until she decided to bring another cleansing.

Falling Star

When you catch a falling star tonight,
Hold it close and hold it tight.
Make a wish before you let it go
Back to the place of ebb and flow.

As you hold the little fallen star,
Remember someone knows just who you are –
A reminder to say you'll be just fine
Let go of the past, then you will shine.

Angels guide and angels see
Your daily struggles to being free.
When you let go of the pain that dwells,
The beat of your heart has a message that tells.

You will be fine and you will learn to trust
You've been loved through those layers of dust.
When you uncover the treasure that lays within
You'll see with new eyes as self-love begins.

This time of pain will help you grow,
Unseen sorrows we can never know.
They help to mould us and make us strong.
When healing begins, we can help others along.

Flaws

In today's world, everything
Has the appearance of perfection:
Perfect face, perfect body, perfect house,
Perfect family, perfect job.

But we are perfect – perfectly flawed.
Just as the potter begins his creation,
Often it becomes not what was intended.
The flaws become something new
And it's molded into something beautiful.

Yes, we are all perfectly flawed,
So embrace your imperfections.
And dare to be yourself,
Not what society says you should be.

Friends

Old friends are the best.
With memories from years gone by,
We remember fun days of youth,
First loves and junior high.

We were all so young and sweet –
In innocence so naïve.
With marriage to our sweethearts
And our purpose we did believe.

We all walked a different path,
And we each have our stories.
We've learned our life lessons
With some regrets and some glories.

We raised our families with devotion
And strived to do our best.
Now we teach our grandkids
About morals and all the rest.

Today it makes my heart just smile
To think about old friends,
Who cherish all those bygone days
Where bonds will never end.

Grand-daughters

They are my joy and such a treasure,
Like angel wings and fields of heather.
It stirs my heart to watch them grow,
As a ray of sunshine on glistened snow.

Little jewels in their roughest form,
The master's creation as is the morn.
My little nuggets so dear to my heart.
Nothing compares to the love I impart.

I will always be here to listen and guide,
A consistent mentor at their side.
With hopes and dreams in our hearts we hold,
They'll one day blossom into the purest of gold.

Healing Heart

I rise above the grief that consumed my heart and soul.
The tears I've shed brought healing in a way I didn't know.
The pain and heaviness were very real.
Your grief is measured by the love you feel.

The wounds of my heart are no longer bleeding.
I have let go of the misery my mind was feeding.
The scars are there and will always be
A reminder that your spirit is now free.

There comes a point when you accept the loss
And move on to the future, regardless the cost.
I know someday we'll meet again,
So I hold onto that promise through all of the pain.

I hear your whisper of love in my ear,
As I silently smile and hold memories dear.
You made such a difference with family and friends.
Tough lessons are learned in the message you send.

Openly love without reservation.
Let it flow freely without hesitation.
One day, our eyes will be opened up wide,
As we watch with our souls, the lives we will guide.

It's time to rise above the pain of the past
And embrace the freedom of release at last.
Let it go to the place of no more sorrow,
With eyes of hope that face each tomorrow.

Hope for Tomorrow

Life is not just filled with pain and sorrow;
Live each day with hope for tomorrow.
Each moment is marked out in time,
As the beat of a heart or sound of a chime.

We all wonder what's beyond the veil,
As our spirit moves on when our bodies fail.
If we could only see what we will leave behind.
Will others say we were loving and kind?

We don't dwell on the things we cannot change.
We just do what we can, even when it seems strange.
We never get to see how the dominoes fall
When we listen to our hearts and answer the call.

We come into this world without a thing,
And we all leave with nothing but death's ugly sting.
Make a difference on the path you're set upon
Like the sunset at night or the shimmer of dawn.

Remember to love yourself, to ignite the flow
Of loving kindness in a world of woe.
Life is not just filled with pain and sorrow.
Live each day with hope for tomorrow.

Hopes and Dreams

When hopes and dreams have been buried,
Don't shovel on the dirt of despair and
    forget them.
Resurrect them into reality.
Nobody knows your dreams but you.

Now it's time to throw in the rope
    of recovery.
All is not lost or forgotten.
Storms don't last forever. They can cause
    damage and destruction,
But they also can bring forth a cleansing
    and a newness of life.

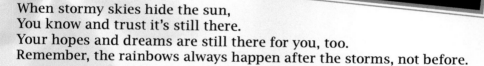

When stormy skies hide the sun,
You know and trust it's still there.
Your hopes and dreams are still there for you, too.
Remember, the rainbows always happen after the storms, not before.

Dreams only die when you decide to walk away and give up.
Storms will come and go; that is for certain.
Now as the skies clear and the sun once again shines upon your face,
Grab onto your rainbow and seek the assurance of brighter days to come.

Life

I'm loving life now, even though it's unpredictable.
Life will always have hills and valleys.
Nothing is certain and nothing is promised.
You never know what tomorrow holds.

When I lost my beloved son,
It changed everything I thought I believed in.
Through years of being lost in my grief and sorrow,
I have learned more about who I am and why I'm here.

I hope his death has changed me for the better.
The impact of it, I believe, has also changed many people he knew.
He touched so many lives in his short time with us
And left an imprint on his friends and family alike.

Don't allow the disappointments to overwhelm your purpose.
Try to keep the toxins out by pouring in good energy,
So you can be a light of hope and love to those around you.
Are you coasting through your life's journey?

Only you can make a difference with the light you share.
A smile, a kind word, a hug or a little encouragement
Can make all the difference in someone else's struggles.
And it makes your own heart smile just to know

You left a little sparkle of light behind.

My Son

There is a very special bond
Between a mother and a son.
The moment that it happened
Was when his life begun.

His first cry brought tears of joy.
It made me forget the pain.
I held him close in wonderment,
As we talked about his name.

His little hands were dimpled,
And his hair soft like silk.
I'd ponder over his beauty,
As he peacefully suckled milk.

He placed his tiny hand in mine
When he could barely walk.
We laughed and we giggled
When he began to talk.

I blink my eyes and now I see
My boy has become a man.
I hesitate to let him go,
But I know this is God's plan.

New Beginnings

Where hope abides, dreams come alive
And sadness no more can reign.
A time has come to ride the waves
Of purpose on which to claim.

If you look for sorrow, it will always be there,
But look for the joy in which to share.
Your wounds will heal when you pay it forward
Without expectations or due reward.

My eyes have opened to see things anew
With clarity and senses to now seek truth.
There's more than you can imagine or ever know
When spirit connects with your inner soul.

Okanagan Heart

As I stand upon this hilltop,
I gaze at the valleys below.
My heart swells for the Okanagan –
With stunning beauty in the life
    that flows.
My heart is here in the Okanagan,
Where wines are red and lakes
    so blue,
Orchards where you can pick
    your fruit:
Cherries, apples, peaches and
    pears, too.

Wineries up and down this valley
Sprinkled with every type of farm.
So much diversity amongst us,
It brings out a pleasant charm.
The lakes are a breathtaking view,
And this scenery is amazing:
Cows about in the farmers' fields
With herds of sheep and horses grazing.

As the sun slowly disappears
Just behind the hill,
I hear coyotes howling
As if to celebrate their kill.
You can hear the crickets chirping now
And the evening prowlers start.
The hoot owl sends a mating call,
As something scurries in the dark.

My favourite part of living here
Is seeing birds galore:
Eagles, hawks and ospreys,
Quail, swans and many more.
There are mountains to ski on
Where the air's so fresh and clean.
Summer days are filled with kayaks, boats and swimmers,
And my Okanagan heart holds this treasure to be seen.

Old Boot

Old Boot got a little laced, down at The Shoe Corral.
Tap Shoes kept the rhythm, jigging for a while.
Stella Stiletto and Sally Slingback also had their fun,
Until they wiggled and wobbled after too much rum.

Two lucky loafers strode up to the bar, all shiny and so new,
While Old Boot polished off a few and began to feel quite blue.
With his soles full of holes, he was feeling rather down.
"I know my boots aren't fancy; my leather is old and brown."

He felt so old and all forlorn, with his laces all untied.
His dear old friend, Plaid Slipper, recently had died.
This made him think of all the years he was well maintained.
He once was sturdy and comfortable 'til left out in the rain.

His whole life he worked darn hard and had no time to play:
Mud-caked memories of smelly socks that took one's breath away.
"If I could be any shoe, perhaps I'd be a cleat.
I'd be of great importance on a famous athlete's feet."

He bid good night to the runners, who sat beside him there.
They were just a couple of heels who didn't really care.
He staggered down the road, with his tongue hanging out.
His eyelets filled with salty tears as he took a different route.

Old Boot had left The Shoe Corral in a sad state of mind
On his journey to a place nobody would find.
He knew he just couldn't go back …
To the second hand shop, on that old shoe rack.

Quiet Time

Sometimes I'd like to sit in the dark
And have some time alone.
Being such a busy mom,
I never have peace at home.

Listen to the drip of the tap.
He works hard; there's never time
For the little things to fix.
Drip, drip, drip, drip.

The clock is ticking loudly.
I never hear it during the day.
Tick, tick, tick, tick
As the time speeds away.

My precious little angels
Are all tucked up in their beds.
Gentle murmurs in their dreams
After stories I have read.

The furnace kicks in with a gentle whir
And my mind is ready for sleep.
All is well with my soul now,
So down the hall I slowly creep.

Drip, drip, tick, tick
Humming and then a whir,
Creaking floors and a snoring spouse –
All is well as the cat does purr.

Self Help

If you can't be yourself
Then who can you be?
There will always be someone
Who dislikes you or doesn't agree.

Be happy with the choices
You make each day.
Be accountable for your actions.
Steer negativity away.

You can change your mind
And your point of view.
Be more open minded.
Acceptance is overdue.

Lonely hearts are hurting
And hopelessness is a disease.
Who will love the unlovely
And save these wounded as they bleed?

Alone I can only be one:
Too big a task to take.
But step by step together,
A solid chain we can make.

Humanity is out of control.
Where does this journey end?
Why can't we give more of ourselves
With a message of hope to send?

Spring-Time

Busy bees and butterflies,
Wispy clouds in pale blue skies,
Cherry blossoms on the trees,
Morning doves coo happily.
So many different shades of green,
Spring has arrived upon this scene.

The smell of freshness is in the air,
And I lay on my swing without a care.
I feel such peace in my backyard,
As the quail on the fence is now on guard.
I read my book in the warmth of the sun.
I'm glad our winter is finally done!

The Bigger Picture

From the ones who just can't thank you enough
For being the heroes when our world was crushed:
Giving comfort to families day after day,
With gentle, loving kindness you portrayed.

Compassion is a gift that you've been given.
To encourage the downhearted, you're empathetically driven.
Sometimes in our sorrow, we forget to tell you
Our appreciation and thankfulness for all you do.

So, I take this moment to give you applause.
Your devotion goes unseen, but you strive for the cause.
Unseen angels cheer us on to do good deeds.
Listen to your heart and you will succeed.

A word of hope, or a hug in care,
When sorrow abounds, you're always there.
Don't be discouraged when feeling low.
You all make a difference – much more than you know.

Deeper Thoughts

Another Year

Another year without you is over
And our hearts are healing still.
There's an empty space where your love once was,
With only memories left to fill.

Each celebration brings up the tears
And the longing in my heart.
You touched so many lives my dear.
And still do although we're apart.

I wish you were still here with us.
I miss your sweetness and your smile,
And your crazy sense of humour
That was your trait and your style.

Happy New Year, my son,
Wherever you are:
On the shores of Heaven
Or upon a distant star.

I'm sending you a big momma hug
Filled with love that never ends.
I miss you my boy, and always will,
Until we meet again …

Love, Mom

Be Still my Soul

As the weeping willow weeps
Beside the still waters,
Still my soul
From the weeping therein.

As the gentle breeze
Causes the leaves to flutter,
May the wind stir within my heart
To ignite it with flames of love.

When my heart is broken
And bleeding with grief,
Let the sorrow of loss
Heal with love and acceptance.

As the soldier stands ready
To conquer his enemy,
Let the enemy fear the unseen angels
Who stand ready beside us.

When the waves of disappointment
Overtake the joy within me,
Let me rise above those waves
To vanquish disappointment with unspeakable joy.

Beyond Myself

Like a bird in a cage, unable to fly and experience my full purpose,
I want to fly above the clouds of foggy confusion and frustration
And search for the peace I am ready to receive.
I want to experience new horizons that make me thirst for more.

I close my eyes and allow the light to shine on my face.
Spirit guides my journey, as the breeze gently lifts my wings
And the breath of life fills my heart with limitless joy and love.
It takes me to a higher dimension of awareness and freedom.

The love that's found is pure and does not limit your dreams
But it encourages you on at your own pace,,
Where you discover dreams become reality
And more unopened gifts await your arrival.

Mother's Love

Who will tuck me in at night and pray on bended knee?
Who will sing me lullabies and bring me security?
I never had a mother who loved the way one should.
She did her job as housewife, and we knew where we stood.

When four more siblings came along, I mothered them you see.
For hugs and cuddles of tenderness, they always came to me.
We grew up without the love a mother should have given:
Hugs and kisses frowned upon as if they were forbidden.

I think a mother spirit came with me when I was born
To bring love to my siblings, instead of mother's scorn.
From deep within I feel I have always had a guide.
How else could I know these things without them by my side?

Perhaps an angel sent by God to show me how to be
A mother to those who need some love and generosity.
A mother's heart, I know I have, with lots of love to share.
I try to guide my children with tender loving care.

A mother's love cannot compare to any other strength.
Her heart bears pain and sorrows of which there is no length.
An encouraging word of wisdom or a funny little smile,
She always knows just what to say and she'll go the extra mile.

Oh Place of Refuge

Laying on the grass, I feel its softness as a blanket beneath me.
I taste the salty sea as it invisibly becomes a mist upon my face.
I quietly listen; the seagulls cry in their greedy search for food.
I can smell and sense the closeness of rain in the air.

Then a sudden little shower cleanses and refreshes all the living.
I can also hear the waves keeping rhythm against the rocks nearby.
The pulse of the earth begins to beat with the beat of my heart.
I close my tired eyes from the busyness I constantly see.

I need to escape for a while, so seek refuge in my mind
From the constant and endless din around me.
I feel and welcome the warmth of a summer breeze
That gently blows the confusion from my mind.

I can taste the saltiness on my lips and feel dampness in the air,
As I relax and let go of the worries of the day.
I am weightless and drift off to a place of peace and light.
This is where I am bathed in the assurance of well-being and love.

I like this place. I feel complete acceptance and freedom.
I feel it as a colour, as a soft orange glow.
And the warmth surrounds me, as I soak in the energy it provides,
As I bathe in complete peace here.

I am now recharged, rested and ready to spread some light,
And I slowly begin to open my eyes ...

I see that the clouds of dismay have gone
And only clear blue skies above me remain.
I feel a cleansing and a refreshing of my spirit,
And my smile is for this new place where I have taken refuge.

I feel the grass on my palms,
As I begin to make angel wings.
Then silently a white feather gently glides
To a landing; its target on my chest.

Open My Mind

My thoughts are going in a new direction.
The excitement I feel is without hesitation.
Open your mind to see things clear.
Open your ears to the message you hear.
You're never too old to learn things anew.
It's a matter of choice with how you view.

If you sharpen your senses they'll stay alive.
With new concepts and visions we can derive.
Keep your energy centered and batteries full.
Empty the toxins, so you don't become dull.
When you cleanse your mind with joy and peace,
Love will flow with a calming release.

Stories Undiscovered

Untold stories are filed deep in your mind, waiting,
Waiting to surface, perhaps in a dream.

Dreams become reality when propelled with intention –
Intentions of bringing those untold stories to life.

Life lessons learned arise from deep within –
Within the corridors of territories unexplored.
Explore some quietness and be still for a while,
While your focus is tuned into calmness.

Calmness will surface, and peace stirs gently the soul.
A soul filled with peace brings a smile upon my heart.

My heart's beat slows and helps me feel refreshed.
Refreshed and renewed as thoughts begin to flow.

Flowing with awareness when I reach that special place.
That special place, where unknown stories do unfold.

Who is She

Who is this woman of wonder?
Most will never get to know the real her;
She only shows herself to those who love her.
Most will think she has all her shit together,
When she is actually having a hard time
Keeping a smile on her face without crying.

She spreads a little love and sunshine wherever she goes
And leaves a sparkle here and there.
The trail she leaves behind does not look
Like the well-trodden path on her heart.
Too many losses and unrepairable wounds
Have left scars nobody knows exist.

Her thoughts and dreams are somewhat lost:
Lost on forgotten wings of sorrow
And vanished on the clouds of disappointment.
Fly away little dreams of hope and purpose.
Perhaps another day you will return.
She wears her mask once again and continues on ...

Wisdom

Don't go chasing honey bees
When the nectar is in the hive.
Don't go chasing rainbows
When the treasure is at your side.

Take a look at what you have
And be thankful for what you see.
Don't wish for what you cannot have;
There's a cost and nothing's free.

Some would say I have it all,
But they'll never know the pain.
Losing loved ones close to you
Brings heart aches just the same.

I'd give up everything I have
Just to have him here.
I'd tell him how much he is loved
And together we'd face each fear.

Just be patient. Don't run ahead.
Enjoy each moment and make it last.
You know not what's around the bend
Or what future plans are cast.

You are left with memories
Of how you loved them so.
Hang on to all the good ones made
And never let them go.

Wings of Peace

My dearest friend makes a difference.
With such admiration and love I feel.
I think of all the pain she has
And her sufferings are so real.

She never complains about her troubles.
Like a soldier she marches on.
I cannot fathom her courageous heart.
In her weakness, she is strong.

Your deepest dreams will fly beyond
The shores of this world's being.
With eyes of sadness your heart will see
The loved ones you are leaving.

Oh gentle lamb, do not despair.
He's prepared a place for you.
Be strong for a little longer.
You'll see His promises are true.

This journey you are walking along
Has been tough and never ending.
With wings of peace, angels embrace
The weak with love unbending.

Your spirit of joy brings laughter
To the multitudes, I'm sure.
Your genuine love is infectious
To thousands, maybe more.

I know you have a mission
To spread laughter and a smile.
An example to always do your best,
Only kindness is your style.

You'll hear His voice when it's time to go
Beyond the heights where love is pure.
Eternal life will be waiting.
There's no pain for you to endure.

Be still, sweet child, and rest in Him.
Your heart will hurt no more.
One day you'll hear Him whisper,
"Come walk with me on Heaven's shore."

Visionary

Ancient Ones

Oh, ancient ones who linger here,
Who guide and watch our being
Help nurture what we can become
And bring utmost inner healing.

Baby steps begin this journey.
Your knowledge will help us grow.
Spirit guides please help us
When channels begin to flow.

Now your voices softly whisper,
"You have almost arrived.
Trust the direction you are headed
And dreams for which you strived."

In due time, spirit guides
Please help for us to see
What assignment we are called for
When you offer us the key.

We'll rest in the assurance of truth and light
As you'll make the answers clear.
We won't wrestle with not understanding,
For your knowledge holds no fear.

We'll fly with the angels upon new heights
Where hearts soar with wings of grace.
We will see beyond the universe
The undying love for our souls to embrace.

Awakening

With open eyes I feel reborn in this body.
I feel like a different person … yet the same.
Messages arise with more meaning than before.
My soul is yearning for a deeper understanding,
And little glimpses of another time begin to make sense.
My time to spread light feels stronger than ever before.
I feel like a babe fresh and new, needing some guidance,
Unsure how to use my gifts that have been idle for so long.

In searching for the right paths to follow … I feel a little lost.
Where do I look? Who will understand what is happening?
Then Spirit places the right people before me.
These are not coincidences but scheduled appointments.
I want to soak up this new ambience; it enlightens my very being.
As I uncover truth from deep within the halls of my spirit,
My inner joy overflows to bring forth clarity of misty dreams
That were tucked away deep inside until the time of awakening.

Nature's Mirror

The promising blue sky looked down and could see
Its reflection upon the clear water and all was well.
The rugged rocky mountain looked down at the water.
He could see he was majestic and he felt confident
And the blue skies behind him gave him assurance.

The pines that grew at the foot of the majestic mountain
Were happy to see they were rooted and secure.
With the rugged mountains that stood behind them
And the beautiful promising blue skies above them.
They grew with strength and fortitude against all odds.

The animals made their homes in the glorious pines
And came to quench their thirst at the water's edge.
The water reflected the security in the pines of protection.
The majestic, rugged rocky mountains of assurance stood
With the clear blue skies of promise above. All was well.

Nature's Symphony

As I lay upon the forest floor,
Soft green moss caresses my core.
I see the leaves flutter in the breeze,
As I look up through the veil of trees.
I hear the bees in a nearby flower,
And see eagles fly with their wings of power.
Oh, to soar upon the wind,
I wish to me his wings he'd lend.
I feel the warmth upon my face
And hesitate to leave this place.

I feel the ants upon my hand
And hear the ducks as they try to land.
A woodpecker keeps a rhythmic tattoo:
Mother Nature's symphony all on cue.
A squirrel chatters in a nearby tree;
He's found his mate and both agree.
It's the little things I can't ignore.
They bring the peace I am longing for.
Oh, be still my soul and you will find
A calmness that renews the mind.

Old Souls

Old soul of mine, I've come to know you
And the secrets you hold within –
Returning back to be reborn
Over and over again!

These visions have such clarity:
One cannot describe.
I am immersed inside a dream,
In this … who can I confide?

I never knew my inner voice
Was such a special gift.
I always had a sense of knowing,
And to my childhood days I shift.

Guardians kept me safe, I knew,
And felt when danger lurked.
Spirit would turn me right around
And keep me from being hurt!

This makes me think of all the times
I listened to that voice
That warned of danger up ahead.
And to me there was no choice!

I thank you for being here
And keeping me from harm.
Old souls know what to expect
And alert without alarm.

Until I have another dream
When I am wide awake,
I will listen to my inner voice
And keep watch on paths I take.

Path Of Peace

If I could find the perfect place
Where peace fills my being,
I'd walk through a forest of green,
As in my mind I'm seeing.

With each mind-step upon the path,
I feel a longing in my soul.
This secret place I've seen before,
And in time it will unfold.

I sense the life and energy,
The deeper in I go.
This path seems so familiar
And my heart just seems to know.

I sit awhile knowing
It'll soon be turning dark.
My eyes glance on a fallen log:
My name carved in the bark.

This path of peace, oh, I hate to leave.
I'll come back another time.
My perfect place, I'll visit you
When I need to calm my restless mind.

Sailor's Demise

As sailors cross the mighty seas,
The tempest storms rage and toss.
It swallows men who dare to sail;
Drowns them to pay the cost.

The waves they roll and winds rise up,
Which churns the depths of the deep.
The weary crew, still strong in mind,
Live the nightmare without sleep.

When strong winds die and waves are calm,
The skies have turned to blue.
The damage assessed, all sigh a relief,
Only one lost from their crew.

Haunted ships from years gone by
Lay on the ocean floor
Waiting to claim the souls above
For the hundreds who died before.

Then once again with tasks complete,
The music begins on deck.
They celebrate their victory
As they sail on above the wrecks.

Then peace returns into the depths
As the ship continues on
Her voyage into unknown waters
To discover what lays beyond.

The Sentinel

The old tree's grown for
   a century – maybe more –
Watching the boats sail just
   beyond the shore.
The light house nearby shines its
   beacon each night,
As the old tree waves in the wind
   at the sight.

His branches are large, thick
   and sturdy.
He's gained respect as
   a tree should, and he's
   became worthy.
He provides the shade on a hot
   summer's day
And houses insects, squirrels,
   robins and the odd blue jay.

He cleanses the air with every breath that he took.
He is as proud of his calling, as is the babbling brook.
Humans admire his great height and girth
And yet they continue to poison Mother Earth.

How much longer must he watch the destruction
From too much pollution and too much construction?
His blackened sap trickles out of his aged rough bark,
As his deep roots send a message to every tree in the park.

Be strong my friends, for I'll soon wither and die.
I'll return to the earth and upon the grass I shall lie.
My time has come and my purpose is done.
Keep spreading your seeds, for one day there may be none.

Widow's Walk

Her one true love has gone away
and forever may be lost.
The captain on a ship at sea
often pays the cost.
Every day she climbs the stairs
to the widow's walk.
She scans the horizon
for the ship she wills to dock.

As years continue on,
it just never seems to end:
Her will to see him coming home,
just around the bend.
Her heart grows weary more each day;
her sad eyes become dim.
She doesn't know how to escape
this nightmare without him.

You will hear her mournful crying,
as you walk along the shore.
It echoes out across the bay
to the one she's searching for.
A haunting wail will stir you up
and make you want to cry.
As you feel her spirit when the setting sun
becomes a midnight sky.

Wounded Soldier

This soldier has been wounded from relentless enemy fire.
His comrades all gave their best,
As they sank into the mire.
"Who will help us now?" he wondered in his head.
So much pain, he felt so weak.
He thought he could be dead.

No turning back, he's trained to fight, no time to hesitate.
"Concentrate on what's ahead.
Push on at any rate."
His eyes can only focus down the end of his gun.
He's a fearless wounded soldier
With the enemy now on the run.

The force he cannot see are the angels there behind.
He breathes a sigh and looks around,
But the battle continues in his mind.
Screaming, blood and chaos, is all he now can see.
The war continues daily.
Nothing can set him free.

His wounds have healed, but the scars run deep.
The body mends,
But his mind doesn't sleep.
Peace will come when he's gone and wars will be no more.
Oh, for him to be free of these earthly shackles,
Just to walk on heaven's shore.

One night a voice calls to him, "Your time to leave has come.
Your purpose here has been fulfilled.
New life awaits beyond the eternal sun.
Your comrades are all waiting, to see you through the gates.
Your journey here is over
And your wings of peace await."

Word Nuggets

A Musician's Prayer

When you are trebled,
Lift your harp to the Lord.
A cymbal prayer at the alto
Will bring harmony and a chord.

When your words are tenor,
His solo voice will chorus your ear.
You will note that His tone
Is not sharp, but soft and clear.

Coyote

A mangy coyote crosses the busy highway
In search of a tasty morsel in the apple orchard.
He's hungry and cares not that humans can see him.
He ignores their prying eyes; their curiosity never lasts.

His mission is focused on survival. His instinct drives him on.
He's in competition with birds of prey.
His eyes are sharp and watch for the slightest movement.
He's quick and comes away with a tasty evening snack.

Music Maker

A song is born when my fingers touch the strings.
The tune in my head is playing without words.
I often wonder how I have created such things.
It brings joy and satisfaction when it's heard.

A master composer must live in my heart,
Feeding me music at night in my dreams.
Songs of life are birthed from the start,
With newly born symphonies it streams.

Quail Watch

They cautiously look around
As they begin to peck.
Slow at first, then suddenly
They all run like heck.

I love the little feather
That sticks up on their head.
"That's where their little brain is,"
I once heard it said.

Their song is like no other.
The males always squawk,
"Coo Cuckoo ... Coo Cuckoo."
That's how quails talk.

I don't know what it means
But the birds all seem to know.
A warning call perhaps,
Or it's mating calls they crow.

So many little chicks
Are so cute to see.
There's always one left behind.
"Oh, please wait up for me."

The mother leads her babies
Into shrubs to hide.
She sees the hawk above them
As he begins his dive.

I guess that's nature's way.
Sometimes it's hard to see.
Survival of the fittest:
That's how it has to be.

Shadow Boxes

When darkness falls upon the hills,
Lights cast a glimmer upon the lake.
Blurred dots of yellow on a canvas of black –
Shadow boxes of houses aglow tonight.

When Does It Stop?

When the music stops,
Do you stop dancing?
When the race is over,
Do you stop running the race?
When your heart stands still,
Do you stop breathing?
When you turn away from something you don't like,
Does it disappear?
When you walk with intent and purpose,
Do you get to your destination?
When you suddenly change your mind,
Is your mind changed?
When your soul feels the rhythm of the rain,
Are you rhythmic?
When you get side tracked,
Have you been derailed?
When you know what your purpose is,
What is the purpose?
When you hang out on the edge of a cliff,
Are you a cliff hanger?
When the questions stop,
Do you have all the answers?

Wishing

When you wish upon a star,
It is not heard from afar.
It is heard from deep within.
When you trust in Spirit,
New buds of hope begin.